ALL-TIME
ESSENTIALS
FOR ENTREPRENEURS

ALL-TIME ESSENTIALS

ESSENTIALS

FOR ENTREPRENEURS

100 THINGS TO KNOW AND DO TO

MAKE YOUR IDEA HAPPEN

JONATHAN YATES

Capstone Publishing Ltd. (A Wiley Company), The Atrium, Southern Gate, Chichester,
West Sussex PO19 8SQ, England
Telephone (+44) 1243 779777

Email (for orders and customer service enquiries): cs-books@wiley.co.uk
Visit our Home Page on www.wiley.com

Other Wiley Editorial Offices

John Wiley & Sons Inc., 111 River Street, Hoboken, NJ 07030, USA
Jossey-Bass, 989 Market Street, San Francisco, CA 94103-1741, USA
Wiley-VCH Verlag GmbH, Boschstr. 12, D-69469 Weinheim, Germany
John Wiley & Sons Australia Ltd, 42 McDougall Street, Milton, Queensland 4064, Australia
John Wiley & Sons (Asia) Pte Ltd, 2 Clementi Loop #02-01, Jin Xing Distripark, Singapore 129809
John Wiley & Sons Canada Ltd, 6045 Freemont Blvd. Mississauga, Ontario, L5R 4J3 Canada
Wiley also publishes its books in a variety of electronic formats. Some content that appears in print may not be available in electronic books.

Library of Congress Cataloging-in-Publication Data (to follow)

British Library Cataloguing in Publication Data
A catalogue record for this book is available from the British Library
9781906465476
ISBN 978-1-90646547-6

Typeset in 11/12pt Frutiger by SNP Best-set Typesetter Ltd., Hong Kong
Printed and bound in Great Britain by TJ International

This book is printed on acid-free paper responsibly manufactured from sustainable forestry
in which at least two trees are planted for each one used for paper production.

CONTENTS

Why You Need This Book
How to Use This Book

WHY YOU NEED THIS BOOK

You bought this book because you have an idea, a great idea that you would like to progress. What you need now is a condensed rundown of everything you need to know and do in order to make that idea happen and to be able to act on it quickly.

As you progress your idea – developing the opportunity you have spotted – you can turn to the hints and tips in this book to help drive you on. A bit like a mentor you can call on whenever you need to, this book will inspire you during the difficult times and help plan your next step when things are going well.

During my own start-up experiences I made many simple mistakes. I also learnt a great deal along the way. I've taken what I learnt as well as looking at what entrepreneurs and inspired thinkers of the past have said, and put together this collection of essential advice that every entrepreneur should know as they start out.

By reading this book as you put your idea into practice, you will avoid making some of the mistakes that entrepreneurs before you have fallen into, and be able to get your idea off and running with a real chance of success.

HOW TO USE THIS BOOK

All-Time Essentials for Entrepreneurs: 100 Things to Know and Do to Make Your Idea Happen has been created based on the understanding that entrepreneurs like to find new and valuable ideas quickly.

Read and digest the information in this book when you have a spare moment, when your head is clear and when you are receptive to innovative thinking. Each page will act as a prompt for further questions. Relate these questions to your business ideas and personal situation, then answer them thoroughly before moving on.

Relax and embrace a single page at a time, thinking about what that particular concept means and how it relates to you and your own business ideas. Be open to changing your perception of the world around you to increase the likelihood of success for your current venture.

Take a quote or an idea from the book and stick it on your wall for a week or two. Then you will have the opportunity to return to something that excited you and think about the consequences of the many different actions you might take now.

This is a manual of ideas, not an instruction booklet. It is up to you to interpret its meaning and relate it to your personal experiences so that you can put into practice new strategies for success.

If you have any questions or ideas you wish to explore, then please e-mail me at *jon@jonathanyates.biz* or I'm on twitter as *Jonathanyates*. I am always excited to hear from people who are willing to take the next step.

START

"Whatever you do, or dream you can, begin it. Boldness has genius, power and magic in it. Begin it now."

Johann Wolfgang von Goethe, 1749–1832

German philosopher and one of the most influential contributors to Western culture.

Begin it now

Take your idea – the one that's been running around in your head, the one you've been telling your friends about – and do something, anything to get it started. Write a description, sketch a prototype, search for similar ideas online or just pick up the phone and call someone to make it happen.

Imagine how the world might be if everyone put their ideas into action. It would be wonderful, exciting and very different from today.

The more you do, the more real your idea becomes. If you talk and act like an entrepreneur, this is what you become.

START

"Work grows out of other work, and there are very few eureka moments."

Anish Kapoor, 1954–

Turner Prize-winning Indian sculptor and philosopher.

Find your eureka moment

The much talked-about *eureka moment* is not a moment at all: it's a length of time that begins with learning and experiences that can be drawn on to realize logical conclusions.

The more you do, the more likely you are to stumble on that elusive intersection between two or more unique experiences.

Everything starts with an idea. Sometimes imagination is more important than knowledge.

Eureka means 'I have found it'. In order to find something you need to be looking for it in the first place. Don't wait around for the light bulb to come on: go and find the switch.

START

"The best reason to start an organization is to make meaning – to create a product or service to make the world a better place."

Guy Kawasaki, 1954–

One of the original employees at Apple, writer and venture capitalist.

Discover your purpose

When you put your heart and real emotion into a venture, the process becomes all the more powerful.

Try to hold back someone dedicated to a cause, be it a business idea or a political course of action – it's almost impossible! These people show an unstoppable attitude that far outstrips their need for financial gain. They have emotion on their side, and an emotional link is the strongest kind.

Innovate with passion and the rewards will come. Be completely involved with your own adventure and see where it takes you.

START

"Art is making something out of nothing and selling it."

Frank Zappa, 1940–93

American composer, electric guitarist, record producer and film director.

Learn to sell the concept

The ability to sell intangible ideas is necessary for all innovators. You may have ideas that are not yet commercially available, so when you are in front of a buyer or investor, sell the concept.

If you have a true innovation, buyers and customers will forgive the imperfections of the prototype. Ask prospective customers to help you create a better product. Companies invest in innovation and early-release products where they can see real competitive advantage.

The opportunity must seem real for the buyer, so take the risk out of the proposition in any way you can.

START

"Some people dream of great accomplishments,
while others stay awake and do them."

Anonymous

Use your time wisely

Time management is a mislabelled skill. What you need to manage is your activity during the time you have. Defining outcomes and physical actions is the core process required to manage what you do.

A simple tool for effective activity management is to prioritize. Ensure you are making the best use of your time right now by doing those things that help the opportunity to grow.

Find the hardest things involved with starting your business and complete them first – then the easier items become even simpler.

START

"I work with wonderful people who support me. And, my beliefs are that the business needs to serve the family rather than the family serve the business."

Kathy Ireland, 1963–

American model, actress, businesswoman and CEO of her own brand marketing company.

Involve family and friends wisely

During the start-up phase your family and friends will be your closest supporters.

But family and friends are not always the best people to approach for views on your business strategy. They really *want* to be on your side and this may cloud their business judgement.

If you do involve your friends and family, make sure that you use them as a sounding board to help you prepare for meetings. Show them the research you're doing and get them involved in helping you with day-to-day activities.

Look to family and friends for financial and emotional support, but remember to listen to their advice objectively.

START

"We can never be certain about the future and therefore we must continue to be flexible and adaptable so that we can react quickly to the needs of our clients and our market place."

Talal Abu-Ghazaleh, 1938–

Called the godfather of Arab accounting, founder of the international Jordan-based professional services organization TAG-org.

7 Be agile

Implement change quickly to take advantage of new opportunities.

Large organizations have lengthy sign-off procedures when implementing new products and services. When starting a business, you have a competitive edge because *you* can make those top-level decisions *now*.

Yakult created a new category of healthy, one-shot, dairy-based drinks. Danone entered the market with the Actimel range and is now the market leader. I'm sure the founders of Yakult are happy with the 10 per cent they now enjoy of the much larger market created by the entry of a blue-chip organization.

"All people are entrepreneurs, but many don't have the opportunity to find that out."

Muhammad Yunus, 1940–

Nobel Peace Prize-winning Bangladeshi economist, founder of Grameen Bank, which provides microcredit loans to developing-country entrepreneurs.

Step out of your career

Are you happy as an employee, making money for other people? Could you take your existing clients and start on your own? Are you ready to find out what life could be if you step into the unknown?

Ask yourself these questions and answer them honestly. If you aren't yet ready for a leap of faith, stay in employment and work hard to earn your salary. Operate your own business in your spare time until you are ready to take it on as a full-time, income-generating job.

START

"A big part of financial freedom is having your heart and mind free from worry about the what-ifs of life."

Suze Orman, 1951–

American financial adviser, writer and television personality. The most successful fundraiser in the history of US television and named by Time magazine as one of the most influential people in the world.

Find start-up capital

'Financial bootstrapping' describes methods of self-financing for your project without external investment. Many entrepreneurs turn to credit cards, bank loans and friends and family to manage their cash flow during start up. Others begin one business to make them enough money to invest in bigger opportunities later.

Some very successful companies were founded on the bootstrapping ethic. Michael Dell started his company with $1000 in capital and grew it into Dell Inc. with the help of $300,000 in loans from close family. In the first year of trading the company grossed $73m by selling customer-tailored PCs through magazine advertising.

What could you start with $1000?

START

"Twenty years from now you will be more disappointed by the things that you didn't do than by the ones you did do. So throw off the bowlines. Sail away from the safe harbor. Catch the trade winds in your sails. Explore. Dream. Discover."

Mark Twain, 1835–1910

American humourist, satirist, lecturer and writer, often referred to as the father of American literature.

Start today

What could be more satisfying than being in charge of your own destiny and answering only to yourself, your employees, suppliers and customers?

You need faith in your abilities and product differentiated in the market. With hard work, tenacity and a little luck, you have the chance to forge your own future.

It's never too late to start implementing your ideas – and it's never too early. You could lay the foundations of a growth business tomorrow, but why not do it today? Someone else could have the same idea and make it happen before you get the chance. It's up to you to start!

IDEAS

"Keep on going and the chances are you will stumble on something, perhaps when you are least expecting it. I have never heard of anyone stumbling on something sitting down."

Charles Kettering, 1876–1958

American inventor, holder of over 300 patents. Founder of Delco Electronics Corporation and head of research for General Motors for 27 years.

You are unique

The collection of diverse events you have experienced during your lifetime is unique to you.

Every day you make decisions about the progress of your life, from brushing your teeth to choosing what task to do first. You are an individual and you make innumerable decisions with infinite outcomes. Explore the way you live your life and question why you make certain decisions – could you do things differently?

Use all of your experiences and connections to find insights and opportunities that no one else has the eyes to see.

You will never, ever meet anyone exactly like you. This is your primary competitive advantage.

"Opportunity often comes disguised in the form of misfortune, or temporary defeat."

Napoleon Hill, 1883–1970

American author who was one of the founders of the genre of personal success and self-help books.

Find problems to solve

Look at products and services and think about the problems they solve. What annoys or upsets people is a source of opportunity: the washer would not have been invented if it were not for a dripping tap.

Many entrepreneurs make the mistake of believing that there must be favourable economic conditions when they're trying to generate ideas, but in a declining economy many problems also need to be solved. High interest rates force people to seek credit management advice. The unemployed need assistance finding jobs. Companies worried about their future growth plans may be able to develop consulting opportunities.

There will always be problems that need to be solved.

"We have two ears and one mouth so that we can listen twice as much as we speak."

Epictetus, 55–135

A Greek Stoic philosopher who taught that individuals are responsible for their own actions and that we have a duty of care to all fellow humans.

Listen to your customers

When selling a product or service, listen to your customers to under-stand their requirements. Customers already have an idea of what they want to buy.

Don't spend most of the meeting telling your clients what you can do for them – you can miss the opportunity entirely. Base your sales pitch on customer-specific needs and tailor an individual solution.

If you are passionate about your product, this will show through even if you have no specific sales training. If there is a market for your product, convey the best solution to meet the client's needs and customers will understand.

A sale is simply a conversation.

"My advice is never to set out just to be rich. Do what you love to do and if in the process you become rich then regard it as a bonus."

James Dyson, 1947–

British designer, inventor of the dual cyclone bagless vacuum cleaner and a fast hygienic hand dryer.

Do something you enjoy

Group your interests and pastimes together and see if there is a way to turn what you love doing into a business. When you enjoy what you do every day, will it feel like work?

If you have a hobby, then start a business around it. You will be more willing to progress and learn than if you're starting from scratch in an industry you don't yet fully understand.

All entrepreneurs work hard and for long hours. If you're going to spend late nights and early mornings on your business, it must be something you enjoy with a passion.

"Skill without imagination is craftsmanship and gives us many useful objects such as wickerwork picnic baskets. Imagination without skill gives us modern art."

Sir Tom Stoppard, 1937–

Multi-award-winning British playwright and screenwriter.

Learn a new skill

If you don't try new things you may never find the roots of your future success.

You may need to learn a particular skill to plug a gap in your business – but once in a while, also be interested in something you would never normally give time to.

Embrace new things away from your day-to-day routine. Try a new sport, research a new industry, go on a course or volunteer to help in a friend's business for a day.

Try fresh and different experiences and grow ongoing opportunities for further unique insights.

"If I have seen a little further it is by standing on the shoulders of Giants."

Isaac Newton, 1643–1727

British physicist, mathematician and astronomer,
one of the most influential scientists in history.

Take a brilliant idea and do it better

You can often find opportunities in existing products that have been around for so long that their failings and costs seem normal to the consumer.

Airlines such as easyJet and Ryanair took the travel industry by storm, offering no-frills air travel at an attractive price. Their flights weren't radically different to what others were offering – they were simply cheaper and delivered access to air travel to a mass market.

The changes you make don't have to be complicated: the simpler, the better.

Build on the advances in technology that others have created to move ahead with your own ideas.

"Imagination is more important than knowledge. For knowledge is limited, whereas imagination embraces the entire world, stimulating progress, giving birth to evolution."

Albert Einstein, 1879–1955

German patent office worker who became the most influential theoretical physicist in recent history.

Harness the power of imagination

17

Children don't seem to be constrained by what they already know and understand. Listen to the stories they create and the make-believe games they enjoy. Where do these ideas come from?

We all had access to our inner child once upon a time, but a sense of conformity creates the need to be accepted as an adult, so we tend to switch off our creative imagination.

Creativity is also stifled at work, especially in corporate environments. Develop your own creativity by reading, drawing, singing and playing games.

If you exercise your creativity then it will be ready to work for you when you need it most.

"Making money is a hobby that will complement any other hobbies you have, beautifully."

Scott Alexander, 1976–

British millionaire and socialite, often cited in the media as 'the most vain man in Britain'.

Appreciate other people's interests

Research a seemingly uninteresting subject right now by purchasing a magazine on an obscure topic. You will always find something you didn't know, which may spark an idea for an opportunity.

If magazines were of no interest then they wouldn't be able to sell copies or advertising space. They have to be interesting to someone, otherwise they would go out of business.

Every pastime or hobby is interesting to the people who enjoy it for a reason; find out what that reason is and see if it can be a benefit to your business.

"Imitation is the sincerest form of flattery."

Charles Caleb Colton, 1780–1832

English cleric, writer and collector.

Protect your ideas

Your ideas need to be protected as soon as possible. Ideas are worth money.

Contact local patent and trademark representatives to learn how to protect yourself from imitation and ensure you have the rights to your invention or idea.

The simplest way to protect your ideas is not to tell anyone until you are ready to launch, unless they have signed a non-disclosure agreement (NDA). Find a standard NDA on the Internet and tailor it to your needs. Once you are emotionally involved with a start-up it can be incredibly difficult to keep it a secret, especially as you will need to begin researching the idea and the market opportunity.

"For a dream to become reality,
make it real enough to believe in."

Peter Jones, 1966–

*British entrepreneur recognized for his lead role
in the UK BBC series* Dragons' Den, *with interests in media,
mobile telecommunications, leisure, property and television.*

Create an elevator pitch

Can you clearly convey your business idea in 5 to 10 seconds?

A good elevator pitch is a set of short statements covering who you are, what you do, and how your goods and services can offer real value to customers. Use this to encourage people to ask you further questions on the nature of the business.

The elevator pitch was created for use during conferences, when you may meet an influential person in a lift and only have the time it takes to travel between floors.

Keep your pitch simple, understandable and concise and it will be a good introduction to your business.

MOTIVATION

"The reasonable man adapts himself to the world. The unreasonable man persists in trying to adapt the world to himself. Therefore, all progress depends on the unreasonable man."

George Bernard Shaw, 1856–1950

Irish playwright, the only person to have received both the Nobel Prize for Literature (1925) and an Oscar (1938).

Be responsible for change

Entrepreneurs embrace change, create change and enjoy change.

Imagine what the world would be like if all the people with brilliant ideas did something with them instead of just talking about them.

Stop moaning that you don't like the way things are – instead, make an effort to make small changes to improve your daily routine.

Change is difficult for many people to embrace because the life they have led so far is comfortable and change causes disruption to routine.

In contrast, entrepreneurs welcome changes from the norm and are excited about the opportunities caused by disruptive behaviour. If you don't create change, then who will?

"The critical ingredient is getting off your butt
and doing something. It's as simple as that.
A lot of people have ideas, but there are few who
decide to do something about them now.
Not tomorrow. Not next week. But today.
The true entrepreneur is a doer, not a dreamer."

Nolan Bushnell, 1943–

*American electrical engineer and entrepreneur, who founded computer company Atari
and the Chuck E. Cheese's chain of pizza restaurants.*

Don't just dream, do it

22

Sitting and talking about your ideas is all well and good, but you need to get out there and do the hard work to make them happen.

This is the part that most people misunderstand. It is easy to find a reason not to take action to make something real.

I hear many, many great ideas every day of the week and you can tell by the person's enthusiasm whether they have a real chance of success or are doomed to failure.

There are talkers and there are doers. The person rather than the idea is the critical ingredient.

Make the hard choice and decide to do, not dream.

"Your mind will answer most questions if you learn to relax and wait for the answer."

William S. Burroughs, 1914–97

American novelist and social critic, member of the Beat Generation and author of Naked Lunch *and* Cities of the Red Night.

Take a day off

Running a business is all consuming of your effort and energy. So take a day away from the office from time to time, and have the discipline to switch off your phone and e-mail.

Go for a walk or enjoy some other activity. Do something completely different to your normal routine.

It's healthy to be away from work and it helps recharge your batteries. It's often in times of quiet contemplation that we generate the best ideas – keep a notebook and pen with you at all times so you can record your moments of genius.

"The real voyage of discovery consists not in seeking new landscapes, but in having new eyes."

Marcel Proust, 1871–1922

French novelist, essayist and critic, author of the seven-part novel
In Search of Lost Time.

Set goals to achieve them

24

Create a collection of pictures and cuttings and set them up in your office or on your fridge to remind you of your grand plans.

There might be a picture of a car, a description of a holiday destination or something representing a deal with a particular client. Always visualize targets specific to your aspirations.

Some people are afraid of setting goals as they might fail to hit them, but by setting goals you are creating motivation. Ensure that your goals have deadlines driving them.

What do you want in life? If you can see where you want to get to, you can plan the best route to get there.

"Every day, you'll have opportunities to take chances and to work outside your safety net. Sure, it's a lot easier to stay in your comfort zone … in my case, business suits and real estate … but sometimes you have to take risks. When the risks pay off, that's when you reap the biggest rewards."

Donald Trump 1946–

Chairman and CEO of property developer the Trump Organization and owner of Trump World Tower in New York.

Enjoy feeling uncomfortable

We are comfortable with experiences we are familiar with. Introduce something new and we feel vulnerable and unable to control the situation.

In contrast, it is vital that you feel comfortable with reinventing yourself in the eyes of your peers.

Many people often enjoy the look of surprise from friends, family and colleagues when they achieve something unexpected. This has happened to me on many occasions during the writing of this book. The reaction seems to be 'You? Writing what?'

Shock value is a powerful emotion.

"Losers visualize the penalties of failure.
Winners visualize the rewards of success."

William S. Gilbert, 1836–1911

*English dramatist, poet and illustrator, best known for
his 14 comic operas including* HMS Pinafore *and* The Mikado.

Visualize achievements

Visualization helps you place yourself in unfamiliar circumstances in advance. When the time comes for you to perform, whether presenting an idea to a forum or signing a business deal, you're some way to being prepared.

When you visualize the goal, try to realize the best outcome. When visualizing the presentation of your idea, create the moment when the audience applauds at the end.

Close your eyes and imagine yourself achieving your goal. Sense how it might feel at the moment of success. Many actors and business presenters benefit from this approach when trying to overcome stage fright.

Always visualize success – then make it happen.

"I felt a strange calmness… a type of euphoria. I felt I could run all day without tiring, that I could dribble through any of their team or all of them, that I could almost pass through them physically."

Pelé 1940–

Brazilian football player, who was given the title of Athlete of the Century by the International Olympic Committee.

Embrace flow

Time seems to drag when you endure a difficult or tiresome task. When you enjoy yourself, time speeds up and the event is over too soon.

Flow is a mental state in which you're fully immersed in a task, often characterized by a feeling of energized focus, full involvement and success during the activity.

If time seems to be ticking slowly by, change your focus. Work on something else, be productive in another area or take a break. You must have absolute focus on the task to drive your idea further.

Capture flow in all your endeavours and you will have the mental aptitude for success.

"Along with a strong belief in your own inner voice, you also need laser-like focus combined with unwavering determination."

Larry Flynt, 1942–

American publisher and head of Larry Flynt Publications, which produces movies and magazines such as Hustler.

Keep on going

There will be times when you want to give up. Humans have an inbuilt fear of failure, but you've come this far, and you need to see your idea through to the end.

Find a mentor, someone who's been through similar experiences and can pass on insights to encourage you. I met with my mentor every fortnight, and his advice every time to "Keep going Jon, keep on going" was a great motivator.

If an issue seems insurmountable, turn it on its head to think about it anew. Often a stunning solution to your difficulty will present itself.

"Some questions don't have answers,
which is a terribly difficult lesson to learn."

Katharine Graham, 1917–2001

American publisher who steered her family's newspaper, The Washington Post,
for more than 20 years and won a Pulitzer Prize in 1998 for her memoirs.

If it was easy, everyone would do it

Starting a successful business is extremely hard and there are many more failures among start-ups than successes. The good news is that the current generation of entrepreneurs is filing more patents, registering more trademarks and beginning more ventures than any previous generation since the industrial revolution.

Remember, the journey to a new business venture requires emotion, commitment, tenacity and dedicated work. It's like riding a roller-coaster – there are deep dark troughs and massive peaks of elation.

Be prepared for both joys and disappointments along the road to your success. It's not easy, but it's worth the effort.

"Motivation is a fire from within. If someone else tries to light that fire under you, chances are it will burn very briefly."

Stephen Covey 1932–

American author who has written several bestselling books on motivation and self-leadership, including The Seven Habits of Highly Effective People.

Find your motivation

Even highly motivated individuals get frustrated, discouraged, or tired at some point.

Everyone needs to know that their efforts are noticed and that their good work is regularly appreciated.

It may not be financial reward you seek but artistic appreciation or the congratulations that come with sporting success. Everyone is motivated by different things. Find out what your own motivations are and use them to achieve the rewards you deserve.

Many entrepreneurs are motivated by the idea of success rather than simply money. What is success to you?

As you employ other people, remember that motivation is a behaviour that you can influence but not create, so find out what your employees' motivators are too.

OPPORTUNITY

"The entrepreneur is our visionary, the creator in each of us. We're born with that quality and it defines our lives as we respond to what we see, hear, feel, and experience. It is developed, nurtured, and given space to flourish or is squelched, thwarted, without air or stimulation, and dies."

Michael Gerber, 1936–

*American author of motivational books and founder of E-Myth Worldwide,
a business skills company aimed at entrepreneurs.*

Find out who you are

- **Altrepreneurs** look for a change of lifestyle and not just increased wealth. Their motivations are not for financial reward but a change of circumstances.

- **Solopreneurs** are individual entrepreneurs, in business for themselves, motivated by money and the achievement of success on their own merit.

- **Entrepreneurs** make money out of ever-changing market opportunities fuelled by the enjoyment of making a profit.

- **Ultrapreneurs** or serial entrepreneurs actively reinvest their money into ever larger business ventures, not solely for financial gain but also for the enjoyment of the process.

"We are what we repeatedly do. Excellence, therefore, is not an act but a habit."

Aristotle, 384–322 BCE

Greek philosopher, the first to create a comprehensive system of thought on morals and logic.

Do the research

You have the idea, now test the market. Conduct face-to-face interviews using tailored questionnaires directly with your target audience.

There are free online services that can help you create online questionnaires and collate the respondents' information into meaningful and beneficial reports. Take a look at:

- www.smart-survey.co.uk
- www.free-online-surveys.co.uk
- www.dotmailer.com

Professional market research companies such as GfK NOP, Ipsos MORI and Gallup will conduct specific research for you – at a price. The benefit of this paid research is that your potential investors will believe it.

Prove that your idea is real by conducting in-depth, professionally presented research showing that the opportunity you've identified really exists.

"It isn't just what you know, and it isn't just who you know. It's actually who you know, who knows you, and what you do for a living."

Bob Burg, 1958–

American author and speaker specializing in entrepreneurial networking and sales skills.

Grow your personal network

Attend free seminars and business functions to meet people from outside your industry. You may find future clients and more effective suppliers among the crowd.

Local business organizations want to grow their own networks by asking people like you to attend their functions. Find out about the BNI, the Federation of Small Businesses and Business Angel Networks in your area.

Register with services such as Facebook, LinkedIn, HubPages, Twitter and Squidoo to grow your professional contacts list and opportunities for your business.

You have the opportunity to spend every morning and every evening networking, so pick and choose the networks that best suit your business needs.

OPPORTUNITY

"Sell a man a fish, he eats for a day, teach a man how to fish, you ruin a wonderful business opportunity."

Karl Marx, 1818–83

German philosopher, political economist and revolutionary, co-founder of Marxism and co-author of The Communist Manifesto.

Take every opportunity

34

If someone asks your advice when they want to purchase a product or service, be bold and say, "Yes, that is something we can deliver for you." Then go away and find a way to do it.

Finding willing clients for your product or service is a time-consuming and sometimes frustrating task. When the opportunity presents itself directly to you, the cost and effort of selling go down dramatically.

Take the opportunity and use your network of contacts to ensure that you deliver what you promise for your new-found client. Do it well to ensure repeat business and unprompted referrals.

"Research serves to make building stones out of stumbling blocks."

Arthur D. Little, 1863–1935

Chemist at MIT who discovered acetate and was co-founder of Arthur D. Little, an international management consulting firm that focuses on technology research.

Read a magazine

Most industries have both trade and consumer magazines full of articles by qualified and experienced writers. Do your research and educate yourself about your own industry.

Reading magazines can provide you with recent updates on what is happening in your chosen niche as well as the specific technical language needed to do business in your industry. If you are able to talk professionally about your new business, you become all the more credible in the eyes of suppliers and prospects.

Your customers and competitors in the industry are reading the same material, so use your new-found knowledge to gain insights, ideas and sales leads.

"Without continual growth and progress, such words as improvement, achievement, and success have no meaning."

Benjamin Franklin, 1706–90

Scientist, diplomat and political writer, one of the Founding Fathers of the United States of America.

Create a scalable business

If you have seen an opportunity to do something better than other people, remember a very important rule: create the solution for everybody, not a product that solves a problem for you alone.

If you're developing a product, ensure that you can produce and sell it in sufficient quantity to enable economic production runs.

A scalable opportunity is exactly what potential investors in your business are looking for. Scalability implies a vehicle for growth as well as a long-term, profitable exit strategy for investors, which is a reason for them to be involved in the first place.

"Let me tell you the secret that has led me to my goal: my strength lies solely in my tenacity."

Louis Pasteur, 1822–95

French chemist and microbiologist, best known for inventing pasteurization, named in his honour.

Be tenacious

Tenacity (*noun*): To hold persistently to something, such as a point of view.

Ensure that you are doing everything necessary to demonstrate your unshakeable point of view, backed up by evangelical zeal.

Outward emotion and passion show your commitment to the project and tie others into the opportunity. Critics will try to dissuade you with thoughts of difficulty and hardship – this is where you have to be strong.

If you truly believe that your idea will work, stand firm, provide your critics with the opportunity to help you and push on regardless. This is your idea and your opportunity to do something with it, so be tenacious.

"Everyone lives by selling something."

Robert Louis Stevenson, 1850–94

Scottish novelist, poet, essayist and travel writer author of
Treasure Island *and* Kidnapped.

Go for larger deals

Compete for large opportunities. Not only will they be a source of higher-value sales, but they will give your business the industry credibility it deserves.

When you find yourself in a situation where a client is too large for you to handle alone, then find a credible partner to work with.

Many start-up software companies have this issue when selling solutions to blue-chip multinationals. They are simply too small to deal with such a large company. The way past this hurdle is to sell your software to respected consulting organizations that have a history with your prospective blue chip and can incorporate your product as part of a broader overall solution.

"I have yet to find the man, however exalted his station, who did not do better work and put forth greater effort under a spirit of approval than under a spirit of criticism."

Charles Schwab, 1937–

US businessman and philanthropist, founder and CEO of brokerage house the Charles Schwab Corporation.

Absorb criticism and use it

You will often face times when your peers criticize your ideas. Use this fantastic opportunity to question their thoughts. What they think could be the foundations of a successful direction for your business.

Many people have thought of business ideas but not put them into practice. Many of your critics will tell you how hard it is to be entrepreneurial and why they did not attempt the next step. Use this negativity to avoid pitfalls in your own venture and remind yourself that you are unique and can get the job done.

Accept help whatever form it takes.

"Even in such technical lines as engineering, about 15% of one's financial success is due to one's technical knowledge and about 85% is due to skill in human engineering, to personality and the ability to lead people."

Dale Carnegie, 1888–1955

American writer, lecturer and creator of courses in self-improvement, selling skills and public speaking. Author of the bestselling book How to Win Friends and Influence People.

Surround yourself with intelligence

40

An entrepreneur should draw on experience gained from knowing a little about a wide range of subjects. In contrast, your employees should be experts in a single subject area, offering you a resource to draw on and a fountain of knowledge.

When starting out you may have a limited number of employees, if any, so seek help from mentors, local government organizations, suppliers or clients to bridge the skills gap.

There are many great-value courses run by government agencies specifically to help entrepreneurs get their ventures off the ground – investigate what's on offer in your area.

OPPORTUNITY

CHALLENGES

"When you confront a problem you begin to solve it."

Rudy Giuliani, 1944–

Major of New York City at the time of the terrorist attacks on the World Trade Center on 11 September 2001. Named as Time *magazine "Person of the Year" in 2002, he was given an honorary knighthood by Queen Elizabeth II.*

Embrace problems

Everyone enjoys games and puzzles that tax our intellect and make us think.

You are taught to solve problems from your school days and you deal with problem solving every day, from what to have for breakfast to managing a route home through rush-hour traffic.

Solving business problems is no different, except for the fact that you may have no previous point of reference or experiences to help you. For example, if you haven't faced an employee's resignation before, it feels a much bigger issue than it actually is.

When faced with a new situation or problem, gather information, research the different choices and make a decision.

"I wanted to be an editor or a journalist,
I wasn't really interested in being
an entrepreneur, but I soon found I had to
become an entrepreneur in order to
keep my magazine going."

Richard Branson, 1950–

*British entrepreneur whose first successful business venture was at age 16,
best known for his Virgin brand encompassing more than
200 companies worldwide.*

When things get tough, keep going

42

The difficulties of starting your own business put many people off from the start and so they don't do it. A little bit of fear can help by giving you clarity of thought and willingness to succeed in adversity, but you need to be able to conquer your fear of failure to ensure business success.

Whatever your natural temperament, you have to become an entrepreneur when you start a new venture. You have to overcome stumbling blocks and seemingly insurmountable problems by using entrepreneurial skills and attitudes.

In times of adversity, focus on the core issues and be persistent.

"I have not failed. I've just found 10,000 ways that won't work."

Thomas Edison, 1847–1931

American businessman and prolific inventor of products such as the gramophone and the light bulb.

43

Learn from mistakes

It is inevitable that you will make mistakes – everyone does – as you haven't experienced all that there is to experience and so you don't have all the reference points you need to make the best possible decisions.

You can only make a decision drawing on your current knowledge, rather than what you don't know.

Every piece of information or situation you take part in adds to your personal library. You draw on all of the memories in your mental database to help you solve the problems you face.

Build on your successes and learn from each failure, making sure that you never repeat it.

"A real entrepreneur is somebody who has no safety net underneath them."

Henry Kravis, 1944–

American financier and investor, co-founder of private equity firm Kohlberg Kravis Roberts & Co, specializing in leveraged buyouts.

Overcome big issues easily

When a complex issue raises its head, find an easy route through it by breaking it down into simpler components.

Start by writing down three things you need to do to get over the problem. Take each of these three solutions and write three ways to achieve it. You can keep on breaking down the issues until they seem manageable and you can begin to solve them.

By following these easy steps you create a solid action plan to follow for any seemingly impossible problem.

"You can get everything in life you want if you will just help enough other people get what they want."

Zig Ziglar, 1926–

American motivational speaker, author of self-help books such as See You at the Top *and* Secrets of Closing the Sale.

Ask for help

When you have a problem with a complex aspect of your business, contact a non-competing company you admire and ask its managers how they would solve it.

Successful people like to help others – and they like to help people who make an effort. They're also often flattered when you come to them for advice.

Every time you contact someone new, you widen your network and you may be able to find out in an instant how to solve some of your current challenges.

"In any situation, the best thing you can do is the right thing; the next best thing you can do is the wrong thing; the worst thing you can do is nothing."

Theodore Roosevelt, 1858–1919

26th President of the United States and also a historian, naturalist, author and soldier. Teddy bears were named after him.

Make a decision

Decision making is not an easy skill to master and often the hardest thing to do in your working day is to commit to a course of action by making a finite decision.

You will inevitably have days where your strategies and tactics don't seem to be working the way you intend them to. Remember that there are forces outside your control that affect your business and influence the direction it takes. You just have to accept this.

Don't be afraid to make a decision when you have to. Be right more often than you are wrong and your business will grow.

"The Chinese use two brush strokes to write the word 'crisis'. One brush stroke stands for danger; the other for opportunity. In a crisis, be aware of the danger – but recognize the opportunity."

John F. Kennedy, 1917–63

Known simply as JFK, the 35th President of the United States was the youngest elected to the office and was assassinated in 1963.

Find opportunity in a crisis

Entrepreneurs enjoy making a profit, and the most successful ones are able to make money out of ever-changing market opportunities.

Markets grow and decline over varying periods. If you're on a city trading floor your opportunity might be measured in seconds; if your business is commercial property development, you're looking at years or even decades.

Successful entrepreneurs are agile enough to recognize and act on opportunities whenever and wherever they appear.

For entrepreneurs, every time is full of opportunities. Find them, seize them and use them to the full.

"Sometimes the situation is only a problem because it is looked at in a certain way. Looked at in another way, the right course of action may be so obvious that the problem no longer exists."

Edward de Bono, 1933–

British physician and author, coined the term lateral thinking and advocates the structured teaching of thinking tools in schools.

Walk around a problem

48

Instead of problem solving, try problem shaping by revising a question so that you can move the issue forward.

For example, the problem might be:

"Why am I unable to find more clients for my seminar series?"

Shaping the question might lead to:

"Why don't clients want to attend my seminar series?"

The answers to these two questions will be very different but they lead to the same goal.

There will always be a way past your issue – you just have to choose and follow the best path.

"One of the advantages of being disorderly is that one is constantly making exciting discoveries."

A. A. Milne, 1882–1956

British author, creator of stories and poems about Christopher Robin and Winnie-the-Pooh.

Learn to adapt and think creatively

49

If a particular course of action isn't giving you the results you want, stop and try a new approach. The trick to successful creative thinking is to be original, ranging widely to light on ideas that are appropriate to the situation you are attempting to solve.

A useful technique to nurture creative thinking is to clear your head of all the ideas you've had before and start afresh with a free mind. This takes practice.

And if creative thinking isn't coming easily to you, don't panic. Panic clouds your judgement and leads to further frustration. Change your surroundings and environment – get away from your normal day.

"An entrepreneur tends to bite off a little more than he can chew hoping he'll quickly learn how to chew it."

Roy Ash, 1918–

Co-founder and president of defence company Litton Industries, director of the Office of Management and Budget under US Presidents Richard Nixon and Gerald Ford.

If you find things tough, that's good

The harder the start-up process, the more likely your idea is to be a true innovation and the harder you should push the opportunity to ensure its success.

Why should a supplier take you on when you might not be able to pay for its service? Why should a client purchase your product when the majority of start-ups go out of business in the first year? Why should the bank give you a loan when your idea is unproven in the marketplace?

Ask yourself the difficult questions before your stakeholders do and come up with answers based on sound business reasoning.

If you had things tough, that's good

MONEY

"Nobody talks of entrepreneurship as survival, but that's exactly what it is and what nurtures creative thinking."

Dame Anita Roddick, 1942–2007

British founder of The Body Shop, a British cosmetics company producing and retailing beauty products that does not use ingredients tested on animals and promotes fair trade with developing countries.

Manage cash flow

Anyone can start a business, but very few people can start a profitable business. The key to success during start up is to manage your cash flow: regular income enables you to grow the business at a realistic rate, particularly if you're relying on your own money.

Many suppliers are willing to help entrepreneurs by deferring payments. Should the business take off, they expect continuing business in return. This is especially true of suppliers who can give their time rather than products, such as creative agencies and designers.

Insist that your invoices are paid on time – and pay your own bills on time too.

"A bank is a place that will lend you money if you can prove that you don't need it."

Bob Hope, 1903–2003

American comedian and actor renowned for his work with the US Armed Forces and numerous tours entertaining military personnel, as well as his humanitarian activities.

Manage spending

When you're starting a venture and income is at its lowest, you need to decide very carefully which products and services to spend your own money on. Use free open source software such as OpenOffice.org, a fully functioning suite of word-processing and spreadsheet tools, and visit www.freecycle.org, a giveaway network for almost anything, including secondhand computers and printers.

Use business card printing websites such as www.vistaprint.co.uk, which provides free services in order to sell you further opportunities when your business takes off.

Rather than taking on expensive employees, outsource work to trusted suppliers.

Another suggestion is to work from home to save expensive office costs.

"Perhaps the very best question that you can memorize and repeat, over and over, is, 'what is the most valuable use of my time right now?'"

Brian Tracy, 1944–

Canadian self-help author who focuses on entrepreneurs and sales professionals, offering talks and seminars include leadership, managerial effectiveness and business strategy.

Work on your business

Take time to work on the development of your whole business, not just running it day to day.

Using your time efficiently is the difference between making yourself busy and running an effective business.

If you are continually doing jobs that need to be done in order to satisfy your customers, then you won't grow. This is working *in* the business – you need to work *on* your business and manage it.

Create a clear strategy forthe promotion of the business as a whole brand, rather than spending all your time on its products and services.

"It has been my observation that most people get ahead during the time that others waste time."

Henry Ford, 1863–1947

American founder of the Ford Motor Company, developer of assembly lines and mass production.

Be an effective organizer

54

As an entrepreneur you need to organize time, people, products, logistics, manufacturing, design and finance. If you can organize yourself, then you certainly have the ability to organize a business.

Getting to meetings on time, paying bills, closing sales and writing letters – you learn these skills throughout your life.

If you can't organize effectively you won't succeed in business. You have to keep on top of those things that need to be done to move your ideas forward and make things happen.

Don't prevaricate, go ahead and do it.

"Repetition makes reputation and reputation makes customers."

Elizabeth Arden, 1878–1966

Canadian businesswoman who founded an international cosmetics business, and was also a major player in American horse racing.

Always ask for more

Ensure that suppliers provide you with the best possible deal. Be creative when asking for something extra. Allow your suppliers to show how valued you are and in return you will maintain your business with them.

Always compare at least three different suppliers by asking for written quotations and references. Take the time to follow up on references to understand who are the best partners for your business.

Ask for return on investment documentation (ROI) as well – detailing the financial benefits you will gain from choosing that supplier. This not only gives the supplier a degree of credibility, but helps you to justify the purchase you intend to make.

Make suppliers work for your business.

"I think this is also a great time to invest in private equity, helping companies grow from the ground up."

Jim Rogers, 1942–

American investor and financial commentator, author of Investment Biker *and* Adventure Capitalist, *and co-founder of the Quantum Fund with George Soros.*

Use the equity you have

In times of financial difficulty, use the equity you have built up as collateral in the business.

Don't be precious with your first business: the key is to get it going and move it forward. If you've done it once then you can definitely do it again.

First-time entrepreneurs exit their first business with, on average, 7 per cent of the company they founded.

It's better to own 10 per cent of a £10m company than 100 per cent of a £10,000 company. Bill Gates owns only 8 per cent of the common stock of Microsoft and still remains the largest individual shareholder.

"Business is other people's money."

Delphine de Girardin, 1804–55

French author, who wrote plays and novels under the name of Vicomte Delaunay.

Use other people's money

Don't use up all of your own financial reserves just in case things go wrong. You may need a fall-back strategy.

There are hundreds of investment groups wanting to speak to entrepreneurs. These include regional investment firms, business angels and government agencies. Approach as many as possible with a solid business plan to see if your idea is worth investing in.

You may be fortunate enough to be offered a substantial amount of start-up capital and then your business will be off and running. At the very least, you gain another perspective on your idea.

"Investors don't like uncertainty."

Kenneth Lay, 1942–2006

American businessman, CEO and chairman of Enron Corporation, best known for his role in the widely reported accounting fraud scandal that led to the company's downfall.

Be what investors are looking for

58

The main questions an investor will ask when thinking about an opportunity investment are:

- Is there a market need for this product or service? Prove this with research and market data.

- Is the product or service commercially scalable? Provide manufacturing or sales data to show how costs diminish with increasing volume in a growth market.

- Do you have access to a good management team? Explain how you do.

- Are you willing to risk your own finances? If so, then you have taken the risk out of the proposition for the investor.

- Are you the right person to make it happen? This is the single most important factor. Are you investor ready?

MONEY

"Security is mostly a superstition. It does not exist in nature, nor do the children of men as a whole experience it. Avoiding danger is no safer in the long run than outright exposure. Life is either a daring adventure or nothing."

Helen Keller, 1880–1968

American author and campaigner for women's suffrage and workers' rights, the first deaf-blind person to graduate from college with a Bachelor of Arts degree and awarded the Presidential Medal of Freedom, one of the US's highest civilian honours.

De-risk the proposition

Limit the risk you ask people to take when investing time and money in you and your products.

Are your goals achievable? Once you have motivated yourself to think they are, then you're prepared to de-risk your ideas for your family, bank, suppliers and customers.

The risk may not only revolve around cost. It could concern confidence in the longevity of the product, consistency of supply or market conditions. Find out exactly what the obstacles are and overcome them so you can move ahead and gain stakeholder involvement.

People don't like to take risks. It's your task to convince them that your proposition has managed and acceptable levels of risk.

"Goodwill is the one and only asset that competition cannot undersell or destroy."

Ludwig Börne, 1786–1837

German satirist and political writer, editor of various liberal newspapers.

Be accountable for your goodwill

Goodwill is a financial term used to describe the intrinsic value of a company that is in addition to its assets – its reputation, if you like.

The goodwill of a business represents the loyalty of both its customers and its suppliers. When investors buy or sell a business, they are not just buying or selling a single piece of land, or a building or the stock, they are also buying goodwill in the form of future order books, repeat purchases, client lists and supplier orders.

Do everything to maintain and grow goodwill between you and your stakeholders.

STRATEGY

"An expert is a man who has made all the mistakes which can be made, in a narrow field."

Niels Bohr, 1885–1962

Danish physicist, first to apply quantum theory and awarded the Nobel Prize for Physics in 1922.

Become an expert

61

Become an expert by writing impartial and informative articles on issues that affect your prospective customers in specific industry sectors. Offer these articles free of charge to newspapers and trade publications to ensure they have a good chance of making it into print.

By creating this kind of launch platform and reinforcing your credibility, you engage the hearts and minds of your stakeholders and create awareness of your in-depth knowledge of the critical subjects for your industry.

Be sure to follow the editorial guidelines of the publications you're targeting and focus on providing helpful information instead of making a sales pitch.

"In preparing for battle I have always found that plans are useless, but planning is indispensable."

Dwight D. Eisenhower, 1890–1969

34th President of the United States and a five-star general, Supreme Commander of Allied Forces in Europe in the Second World War.

Stay in control

Keep control of your business focus by continually monitoring and reassessing your long-term plans.

Problems have a habit of snowballing. If things start to get out of control, you lose business momentum and end up firefighting problems instead of providing solutions that help your business grow.

Not being in control quickly becomes time consuming and costly to future business success. So ensure you get back on track as rapidly as possible.

The more you do, the more there is to be done – so be clear about your objectives and growth strategies so that you retain your focus.

"Advertising is about norms and values,
aspirations and prejudices. It is about culture."

Anil Ambani, 1959–

*Indian businessman awarded Entrepreneur of the Decade
by the Bombay Management Association and
MTV Youth Icon of the Year in 2003.*

Create a unique business culture

Invest emotion to the products and services you offer. Create a culture of words and pictures and an identity that customers and partners can tap into.

The world loves a quirky business, one that is founded on fun but with a serious business heart.

Look at how Google advertises job opportunities:

> Top 10 reasons to work at Google – number 3: "Appreciation is the best motivation, so we've created a fun and inspiring workspace you'll be glad to be a part of, including on-site doctor and dentist; massage and yoga; professional development opportunities; on-site day care; shoreline running trails; and plenty of snacks to get you through the day." *

When you create a unique culture you foster the involvement for all your stakeholders.

---

* Reproduced with permission of Google.   **STRATEGY**

"The difference between ordinary and extraordinary is that little extra."

Jimmy Johnson, 1943–

American football coach and broadcaster, author of Turning the Thing Around:
My Life in Football.

64 Break constraints

Your business may make money from methods and practices that maximize economies of scale to produce products in a tried-and-tested manner – your suppliers aim to do the same. When you want to try something different they often seem disinterested and unwilling to help.

Try not to be constrained by existing practices. Push to get exactly what you want and the products you require to start your business and satisfy the market demand you know exists.

Compromise may mean the death of your innovation, so find a way to get exactly what you want.

"The knack of flying is learning how to throw yourself at the ground and miss."

Douglas Adams, 1952–2001

*English novelist and dramatist , best known as the author of
the* Hitchhiker's Guide to the Galaxy.

Try something completely different

Expand your experiences by trying something completely different and outside your normal comfort zone.

Join a group, try a sport, take a course, watch a film, try some new food, buy a different book, call a company you admire, wear different clothes, take a car for a test drive or do some volunteer work. You must immerse yourself in a new pursuit to expand your capacity for creative thinking.

All of these activities will give you insights into other people's worlds, push the boundaries of your own experiences and provide you with pathways and connections to new opportunities.

"Keep your friends close,
and your enemies closer."

Sun Tzu, 544–496 BCE

Chinese author of The Art of War, *a hugely influential ancient book
on military strategy.*

Keep competitors close

66

Get to know your competitors in both a professional and a personal capacity. Competitors are a good source of new customers. In many instances competitors may actually contact you directly, as there may be a need for you to help them with backlogs and overflow business, or with specialized services they are unable to offer.

This works the other way around when you offer a service for the first time and need to ask help from a competitor to get the business closed and retain a client.

Knowing what your competitors are planning helps you organize for the future.

"Refusing to ask for help when you need it is refusing someone the chance to be helpful."

Ric Ocasek, 1949–

American musician, formerly vocalist of The Cars and a producer for several other successful groups.

67 Outsource

You may surprise yourself at the ease with which you overcome many new challenges. However, when you do recognize the need for skills you lack, outsource to find complementary expertise.

Stick to these three golden rules for best practice:

1. Look for a business partner, not just a provider.

2. Set and agree clear goals, objectives and expectations.

3. Develop a business relationship based on mutual trust.

Eventually you may be able to afford to bring the relevant function in-house and run it yourself.

Some very affordable and expert business service companies exist, so look for the right one for your business.

"Business is like riding a bicycle.
Either you keep moving or you fall down."

Frank Lloyd Wright, 1867–1959

*Architect and interior designer, termed the greatest American architect of
all time by the American Institute of Architects.*

Call someone right now

Pick up the phone and call someone you respect in business or your industry to introduce yourself and your products.

Ensure that your conversation has a reason, is relevant and personalized, and you may find yourself a new client, a new member of your personal network, some fresh information on the industry you work in or someone who can pass on your details to interested contacts.

Networking has an important place in your business. Find someone in your network you haven't yet met and ask them to lunch, so you can find out what they do, how it relates to you and how you can help each other.

"Doctors and scientists said that breaking the
four-minute mile was impossible, that one would
die in the attempt. Thus, when I got up from
the track after collapsing at the finish line,
I figured I was dead."

Sir Roger Bannister, 1929–

British athlete best known as the first man to run a mile in less than 4 minutes,
also a neurologist and Master of Pembroke College, Oxford.

Move the boundaries

69

You may make a request of a supplier and they say, "We don't do it like that." Ask them why not – it may be they've never been asked before. You don't want to be pulled down a route that satisfies a supplier's solution rather than your own requirements.

Make sure that you stick to your original product specification however hard it seems at the time.

Difficulty in creating a new product or service means one of two things: either there is no market need, or you have hit on a true innovation. If you're sure it's the latter, pursue your idea relentlessly.

"The way to get started is to quit talking and begin doing."

Walt Disney, 1901–66

Multiple Academy Award-winning American film producer, director, screenwriter, animator, voice actor, philanthropist and entrepreneur.

Do it better than the competition

70

Whenever you're applauding a person, a product, a service, an idea or an achievement, always ask yourself: 'Could I do it better?' If the answer is yes, then go and do it.

When your competitors come out with next-generation offerings, find a way to regain the advantage. Continually question the relevance of your core products and services so that you stay ahead of the market.

First-generation MP3 players held a reasonable and growing portion of the portable music player market for four years. Then the Apple iPod was released. Can you name five other MP3 players?

Don't just keep pace with competitors, lead them.

MARKETING

"If you do build a great experience,
customers tell each other about that.
Word of mouth is very powerful."

Jeff Bezos, 1964–

*Founder of online retailer Amazon.com and of human spaceflight venture
Blue Origin.*

71
Evangelize your services

If you're unable to get excited about your services, how can you expect your customers to become excited about them and spread the word on your behalf?

Use your own products and services every day. Eat, live and breathe your business — be the most devoted user of your products.

Be your most critical customer in order to test the product and the customer services you offer. Step away from the business and look back as a customer rather than an owner.

Then you can be a real evangelist for what you offer.

"And I'm not an actress. I don't think
I am an actress. I think I've created a brand
and a business."

Pamela Anderson, 1967–

Canadian-born actress, glamour model and entrepreneur.

Create a brand

If you can answer the following two questions, then you have a true brand: What is the point of your products and services? Why should anyone care about your business? Create your brand identity around your answers to gain a loyal customer base.

Why do we buy products from The Body Shop? Is it because they are better products or because the company embodies fair-trade ethics? In fact it's a combination of both through marketing materials and press coverage that are carefully moulded to create a cohesive brand.

A brand is developed and nurtured through all customer interactions, so take care to ensure that all your messages are consistent.

"Attitudes are contagious. Is yours worth catching?"

Anonymous

Create customer involvement

73

If a customer feels involved with a company then they are loyal to its products or services.

Actively involve your customers in all aspects of your business: get them talking about it and keep them emotionally connected with regular communication through newsletters, phone calls, personalized e-mails, competitions and questionnaires.

If you go to Fruit Towers, the head office of smoothie maker Innocent, you can sit down, relax and try one of their new drinks. Innocent actively invites you to do this on each and every bottle. In reality only a handful of people turn up each year, but the invite is there to make customers feel welcome and part of the Innocent experience.

MARKETING

"One of the deep secrets of life is that all that is really worth doing is what we do for others."

Lewis Carroll, 1832–98

Pen name of British author, mathematician and inventor Charles Dodgson, creator of literary nonsense novels Alice's Adventures in Wonderland *and* Through the Looking-Glass, *as well as poems including 'Jabberwocky'.*

A brand is a promise

74

If you can consistently deliver the ideals of your brand to the expectations of your customers, then they will consistently buy into your brand identity.

A brand is a contractual promise between a company and its customers. Each time customers consume the product or experience the service, they know it will be just as brilliant in terms of satisfaction, experience and quality.

Look at recent 'Mac vs PC' adverts. In Apple's adverts its computers are portrayed as fun, up to date and part of your digital life; the PC as a stereotypical business machine. Microsoft is fighting back with its 'I'm a PC' campaign featuring ordinary people and celebrities using its products.

"I have always loved the competitive forces in this business. You know I certainly have meetings where I spur people on by saying, 'Hey, we can do better than this. How come we are not out ahead on that?' That's what keeps my job one of the most interesting in the world."

Bill Gates, 1955–

American businessman, philanthropist, author and founder of software company Microsoft.

Punch above your weight

Compete at a level above even your expectations to achieve greater rewards. Position yourself alongside leading products and services to gain credibility by association.

By placing yourself in circumstances that motivate you to work harder, perhaps in a larger market, you will move your business forward exponentially.

Retailers are extremely effective at developing own-label products that are remarkably similar to premium brands. The look and feel of the products are the same and they share the same shelf space, but the own-label products are usually better value for money. The trick is the association: the retailers' own products benefit from the marketing spend of the premium brands.

"The world is more malleable than you think and it's waiting for you to hammer it into shape."

Bono, 1960–

Stage name of Paul Hewson, lead singer of Irish rock band U2, activist on African issues and co-founder of socially conscious initiatives EDUN and Product Red.

Create a buzz

Word-of-mouth is a very powerful marketing tool that every entre-preneur must learn to use. It can be low cost and even works when you sleep.

Viral marketing ocours when customers endorse a product or service that they admire and pass on that information to those most likely to be in the same market.

Talk to friends, educate opinion leaders, pitch a story to the media, send out an e-mail newsletter, run a competition or start a blog. Encourage your customers to do the same. Learn about viral mar-keting techniques and make them work for you in a positive way.

"If we want a love message to be heard,
it has got to be sent out. To keep a lamp burning,
we have to keep putting oil in it."

Mother Teresa, 1910–97

*Albanian Roman Catholic nun with Indian citizenship who founded
the Missionaries of Charity in Calcutta and gained world renown
as a humanitarian for the poor and dispossessed. She won
the Nobel Peace Prize and was beatified by Pope John Paul II
as Blessed Teresa of Calcutta.*

Make yourself heard

Don't shout to be heard, communicate cleverly with consistent messages that rise above the background noise of your competition.

Use your unique qualities as the launch platform for your marketing communications. Write the story of how your idea was born as a press release, to encourage emotional links with your customers around the hardships and successes of your journey.

Richard Branson hit the headlines when it was announced that the aircraft Concorde was being scrapped. He simply asked his PR agency to spread the word that he would buy the Concorde fleet from BA for £1. This arrogant but brilliant story gained Virgin massive points over BA and secured Branson's brand image as the people's entrepreneur.

MARKETING

"You now have to decide what 'image' you want
for your brand. Image means personality.
Products, like people, have personalities,
and they can make or break them
in the market place."

David Ogilvy, 1911–99

British advertising executive, whom Time *called 'the most sought-after wizard
in today's advertising industry'. His agency developed campaigns
for companies such as Schweppes and Dove and he was famous for
his statement 'I hate rules'.*

Create a family of products

When you've found success with your first product or service, augment its appeal for a different target market.

Range extension may be as simple as repackaging or repositioning the product for an alternative audience or even another industry.

Have a look at Microsoft Office products, first built for business and then rebranded for various user groups: Office Professional, Office Home and Student, Office Small Business, Office Standard.

Loyal customers will also support your new products if you can offer relevant range extensions and provide reasons for them to upgrade to a newer version.

Extending your range could be a straightforward and effective growth strategy and enable you to move into other markets.

"Be very, very careful what you put into that head, because you will never, ever get it out."

Thomas Cardinal Wolsey, 1471–1530

English statesman and Roman Catholic cardinal, Lord Chancellor to Henry VIII and skilled international diplomat, stripped of office after he failed to obtain a divorce for the King from Catherine of Aragon.

Create your own PR

Every business needs publicity to spread the word. Effective public relations helps you gain new business as well as building trust and credibility.

Prepare a press release, use free PR distribution services and pick up the phone to newspapers and magazines that offer relevant editorial coverage for your customer base.

Editors like to hear real-life stories from the founders of a business. You might talk about how you secured a new client or hired a new employee for the business. Work with local papers to get local coverage and grow your experience and press release writing skills before you attempt to go national.

"It is not the strongest of the species that survive, nor the most intelligent, but rather the one most responsive to change."

Charles Darwin, 1809–82

British naturalist and geologist who developed the theory of natural selection, the foundation of modern evolutionary theory, and was the author of On the Origin of Species *and* The Descent of Man.

Be positively disruptive

Create disruption in the field in which you want to be heard. Adopt a maverick approach and change the way people do business in your chosen industry. Create a buzz about your ideas by telling the press what you're doing that's new.

Xerox marketed the first mouse for personal computers, but did not promote the technology because it feared possible future losses to its paper copying business. In contrast Apple, which began as a computer company, has continually reinvented both its hardware and software and developed radically new products and markets.

Most people resist change – as an entrepreneur you need to create it.

SALES

"Formula for success: under promise and over deliver."

Tom Peters, 1942–

American writer and management consultant, best known for co-writing worldwide bestseller In Search of Excellence.

Under promise and over deliver

If you continually exceed your clients' expectations, they have few reasons to look at your competitors.

Think of subtle ways to add value for your customers. For example, a car dealership can deliver your new vehicle with a bouquet of flowers on the back seat as a special unexpected gift. In an instant the dealership generates a wealth of goodwill at a small cost.

The possibilities are endless. Use a little creativity to ensure that your customers get more than they expect in a positive way.

Be careful not to set expectations too high, as you must consistently deliver. If you fall short of customer expectations then the penalty is a possible loss of business.

"No matter what your product is,
you are ultimately in the education business.
Your customers need to be constantly educated
about the many advantages of doing business
with you, trained to use your products more
effectively, and taught how to make
never-ending improvement in their lives."

Robert G. Allen, 1948–

Canadian-American writer on financial investment, author of Nothing Down
and co-author of The One Minute Millionaire.

Sell benefits not features

82

All products and services are solutions to everyday problems. Your customers don't necessarily need to know how you're going to solve these problems, just that you are.

Try to sell the features of tap water: a cold combination of hydrogen and oxygen in a liquid state. Not a very appealing product. People may be put off by the technical words. But if you promote tap water as an environmentally friendly, refreshing, free soft drink that helps you rehydrate, quench your thirst and keeps you cool, then you are solving their problems.

Create the foundations of your sales pitch by saying what your product or service is and how it solves a specific problem.

"Living on Earth may be expensive,
but it includes an annual free trip
around the sun."

Ashleigh Brilliant, 1933–

British author and cartoonist, best known for Pot-Shots, *a comic of illustrated epigrams,
and for books such as* I May Not Be Totally Perfect,
but Parts of Me Are Excellent, and Other Brilliant Thoughts.

Generate goodwill

Customers who receive an unexpected bonus when doing business with you always remember that you went further than the competition.

Consumers' expectations of dealing with businesses are much higher today than a few years ago. Customers are aware of value and good service and are willing to let you know when you've let them down.

Try a buy-one-get-one-free offer or take a client out to a smart restaurant. Arrange for your top 10 customers to meet up for a free networking seminar. Distribute insights into your industry.

Do things that set you apart – your competitors may be doing the same, so be creative.

"In sales, a referral is the key to
the door of resistance."

Bo Bennett, 1972–

American entrepreneur, motivational speaker and author of Year to Success.

Ask for a referral

When you provide customers with prompt and reliable quality of service, they'll be happy to spread the word on your behalf, often without you having to ask.

When a customer compliments you on your work, ask them to put it in writing for you to use as a testimonial in your marketing material.

After every sale, ask the customer why they chose you over the competition. This is simple ongoing market research. If you sell fast-moving goods, create a reply-paid postcard for buyers to fill in as part of a prize draw. Use the information they supply in your literature and press releases. You'll be pleasantly surprised how effective this becomes with practice.

"If it's free, it's advice; if you pay for it, it's counseling; if you can use either one, it's a miracle."

Jack Adams, 1895–1968

Canadian professional hockey player who spent 36 years as coach or general manager of the Detroit Red Wings and became president of the Central Hockey League.

Provide free advice for customers

Create a seminar that's informative for your client base. Use this forum to communicate the availability of new products and services.

Ask one of your clients to be a keynote speaker on a critical element of the industry. They will feel honoured that you've chosen them over other clients.

Keep costs down by offering web-based seminars. One company I know provides fortnightly introductions to its products online. It e-mails a form to prospects and asks them what they would like for breakfast – the food arrives at their desks at 8.30, just in time for the online seminar to start. This has proved a very successful method for getting people involved in the business.

Do unforgettable things and your customers won't forget you.

"The best teamwork comes from men who are
working independently toward one goal
in unison."

James Cash Penney, 1875–1971

American businessman and entrepreneur, founder of J.C. Penney stores.

Make yourself part of the team

Demonstrate that you are there to help your customers increase their profits and solve their business problems. Become indispensable to your customers and they will start to call you for advice rather than you calling them to sell.

Your ideas may save the day in a difficult business situation. Link your concepts and problem-solving skills with your products and services and you have the ability to consult for your clients.

The more integrated you are with your customers' businesses, the harder it will be for a competitor to move in on your territory.

"Be everywhere, do everything, and never fail to astonish the customer."

Motto of US retail chain Macy's

Create excellent customer service

Keep customers coming back by making sure that your products or services work well for them. If their problems persist, show concern and provide new solutions at your own cost.

If you are the owner of the business and an issue arises with your products or services, then go out and see the client. You are the one in control and the customer will appreciate the time you have given up to compensate for the problem and help solve it. You are responsible for ensuring your customers' satisfaction.

"A friendship founded on business is better than a business founded on friendship."

John D. Rockefeller, 1839–1937

US industrialist and philanthropist, founder of the Standard Oil Company and the first American billionaire.

Don't have clients, have friends

Business is done by people. Meet your stakeholders and customers outside the work environment and develop a personal rather than simply a business relationship.

This sounds a difficult step, but it is necessary to forge social relationships in order to maximize your business relationships.

Many organizations entertain customers and prospects at golf days, racing events or shoots. Corporate events are time away from the business with those you do business with. Scale this idea down to suit your own customers.

Invite prospects to local events. Even if they turn you down on this occasion, they won't forget that you invited them.

"I have never worked a day in my life without selling. If I believe in something, I sell it, and I sell it hard."

Estée Lauder, 1906–2004

American co-founder of the cosmetics company that bears her name, the only woman on Time magazine's list of the 20 most influential business geniuses of the twentieth century.

Ask for the business

89

A sale is a just a conversation. Talk to your prospects and answer any questions they might have. When the time is right, ask for the business. The customer can only say no.

If you do get a rejection, find out what their objections are and try to overcome them. When you ask for the business a second time, the customer should have little reason to say no.

You need continuing sales to survive, so if a prospect persistently turns you down, waste no more time, move on and find a more committed client.

"Let us move from the era of confrontation to the era of negotiation."

Richard M. Nixon, 1913–94

37th President of the United States, the only American president to resign from office following his role in the Watergate scandal.

Negotiate every opportunity

When you're buying and selling, you're trading. Negotiation ensures that trading is fair.

Be creative with your negotiation and don't haggle over price. You could offer a discounted service contract or a free annual health check for your offering instead. Cash is king. Keep the price high to maximize cash flow and offer other items that you can afford to give away.

Negotiation isn't about beating the other party into submission. The key is to enable both parties to feel mutually satisfied that they have both gained from the process – a win–win situation.

SUCCESS

"Being a top athlete requires total concentration. And some sacrifices. I have suffered a great deal, but here's the result. Never give up, make your dreams come true."

Alain Robert, 1962–

Know as the 'Human Spider', Frenchman Robert has scaled 85 skyscrapers including many of the world's tallest buildings, most without ropes or assistance.

Adopt the right perspective

91

During the start-up phase of your business emotion is a powerful ally, but in times of success and failure it can confuse you. So remember: things are never as good or as bad as they seem at the time.

Listen to your heart and you will know the right level of appreciation for any given situation. Allowing yourself to lose a piece of business might be a better prospect than fighting for it; conversely, winning a new piece of business might mean over-expansion during a difficult economic time.

Keep everything in perspective. Take a step away and look back at the real situation – be objective rather than subjective.

"The only place where success comes before work is in the dictionary."

Vince Lombardi, 1913–70

American football coach, head coach of the Green Bay Packers and famous for his motivational skills and commitment to winning.

Hard work pays off

Two thirds of the working population would rather be doing something else instead of their current job. How hard do you think these people are working for the organizations that employ them?

Find some self-employed entrepreneurs and ask them whether they enjoy their work. The answer will most likely be that the work is very hard and the hours are long, but the rewards, both financial and social, are fantastic and going to work is something they look forward to every day.

There are few shortcuts to success, but looking for them is one way to make your hard work go further.

"Some people fold after making one timid request. They quit too soon. Keep asking until you find the answers. In sales there are usually four or five 'no's' before you get a 'yes'."

Jack Canfield, 1944–

American motivational speaker and success coach, co-creator of the Chicken Soup for the Soul *book series with Mark Victor Hansen.*

When people say 'no', ask again

93

If your customers are putting up barriers, find out why – their implied negativity may not always be founded on what you expect.

You need to have the ability to appreciate and empathize with an objection before you can overcome it.

Perhaps you think it's a fatal cost objection, when it may simply be a cost objection during this budget phase. You don't yet know what you don't know, so ask.

Remember, in business it's much easier to say no. Be bold enough to ask difficult questions and challenge the answers you get with creative reasoning.

"I've always worked very, very hard,
and the harder I worked, the luckier I got."

Alan Bond, 1938–

*British-born Australian businessman, property developer and founder of
The Bond Corporation, who was awarded Australian of the Year for bankrolling a
winning America's Cup yachting challenge.*

Create your own luck

Luck and chance play important roles in your success.

However hard you work there will be times when things naturally fall into place with very little effort. In most cases this is simply the culmination of all the activity you have invested in growing your company.

Even if you lose a sale, stay in touch with the prospect and offer to help in the future. You will be next in line should the competitors products fail to deliver.

We all know people who are naturally lucky, but the people who make things look easy are often those who work the hardest.

"A journey of a thousand miles starts with a single step."

Lao Tzu, c. 600 BCE

Chinese philosopher, author of the Tao-Te Ching, *the most frequently translated text after the Bible.*

Enjoy small successes

Small successes are the building blocks of large achievements. Jump from each little win to the next and grow in confidence during your business journey.

Celebrate new contracts, new employees, new customers – and the fact that it's Friday. Celebrate the anniversary of the birth of your business and ask your customers to join in.

When things aren't going your way, remember these small triumphs and how you went about achieving them to ensure that you have enough confidence to overcome trivial issues.

Each step you take is a step nearer your goal. If you stand still you will never get any closer.

"Sometimes the questions are complicated and the answers are simple."

Theodor Seuss Geisel, 1904–91

American author and cartoonist, best known for his collection of children's books written under the pen name Dr. Seuss, such as Green Eggs and Ham *and* The Cat in the Hat.

Create solutions to problems

96

If you can solve a problem that millions of people suffer from, then you have both a product and a market.

James Dyson saw a problem with vacuum cleaners and found a way to overcome the time, cost and mess endured when changing bags full of dust and household dirt. By doing away with the bag, Dyson solved a simple problem with complex technology and packaged it as a straightforward solution for the consumer.

Find out what frustrates people and see if there's an opportunity for you to create a better way of getting things done.

"Part of the issue of achievement is to be able to set realistic goals, but that's one of the hardest things to do because you don't always know exactly where you're going, and you shouldn't."

George Lucas, 1944–

Academy Award-nominated American film director, producer and screenwriter, creator of the Star Wars *saga and the* Indiana Jones *films.*

Set realistic, achievable goals

There's nothing more frustrating than failing to achieve a personal goal for reasons that are beyond your control. It's the same with business goals.

Always set goals that you can realistically achieve within a set time period and over which you have as much control as possible.

Making £1m in 12 months is not easily achievable: try making £1m in 5 years instead. How do you go about this? Where do you start? What goals can you set to guide you on the path to this larger aspiration?

Set small but achievable goals to boost confidence with small but meaningful wins.

"Every worthwhile accomplishment, big or little,
has its stages of drudgery and triumph;
a beginning, a struggle and a victory."

Mahatma Gandhi, 1869–1948

*Political and spiritual leader of India and the Indian independence movement, whose
birthday, 2nd October, is celebrated as a national holiday and
the International Day of Non-Violence.*

Rise to the challenge

98

There will be challenging times in any business, but particularly in a start up. It is imperative that you focus on the task you have set yourself. There will be times when competitors outflank you or when nature conspires to disrupt your business. These challenges are mostly outside your immediate control.

Learn from disasters and work them to your advantage. Some people take the easy route back to their former lives if things go wrong. Have the courage to strive and persevere in order to succeed and create a different world for yourself.

"Entrepreneurship is living a few years of your life like most people won't, so that you can spend the rest of your life like most people can't."

Anonymous

Do everything to make your idea real

You have decided to start your adventure. This is an opportunity to create your own destiny from the start and on your own terms.

There are few hard-and-fast rules in business, so you need to do everything and anything to make your business a success. If you invest time, money and emotion into your business it will come alive.

You are the greatest advocate of your business, so live and breathe your product or service to show the world how enthusiastic you are about it.

"The greatest reward in becoming a millionaire is not the amount of money that you earn. It is the kind of person that you have to become to become a millionaire in the first place."

Jim Rohn, 1930–

American entrepreneur and speaker on personal development.

100 Become an entrepreneur

What type of person do you need to be to achieve success? Are you a born innovator or do you need to learn the rudiments of entrepreneurship first?

The adventure of founding your own business is about more than money, it's a personal challenge. You may want to work for myself, you may want to work hard for a few years and then relax, or you may want to change the way the world works. Whichever applies to you, be bold.

When you act like an entrepreneur, by doing and saying things that move your idea forward, people will see you as an entrepreneur.

You're not born an entrepreneur, you become an entrepreneur.

ABOUT THE AUTHOR

I founded my first business, Santeau, in April 2004 in my spare room and after some very hard lessons sold my 75% majority stake in September 2007. My idea was simple: find a new way to help people drink more water. I invented a vitamin-enhanced flavor burst for bottled water called O2GO and extended the range to include a new product called Wahoo. These products currently sell into the military and retail markets. I still work with the Santeau business every day and enjoy watching the business grow. I started with a modest budget and a naïve but resounding belief in my new inventions. This insider's view gives recognition to the hardships and success involved in launching a business innovation from scratch without looking back through rose-tinted glasses.

In order to stretch my own horizons I undertake a new endeavour every year. In the past decade I have run the London Marathon, completed a three-year drama course, competed in the Olympic-distance London Triathlon, lost 35 pounds in weight (twice), trained for the Marathon Des Sables, written a book, learnt how to play squash, started Nordic walking, gained my motorbike licence, taken an Open University degree in Planetary Science, shared a stage with B-list celebrities, met amazing people and numerous other achievements.

I do these things because I enjoy the challenges and rewards they bring.

I have been called a high achiever, an inventor and a maverick. I consider myself to be a normal person with a drive to experience new things and work hard to ensure I get the best results. I wish I had known it was that simple at school.

The following quote by JFK encapsulates my ideals perfectly:

We choose to go to the moon in this decade and do the other things, not because they are easy, but because they are hard, because that goal will serve to organize and measure the best of our energies and skills.

Praise for Jonathan Yates:

It won't be long before he gets a loyal following.
Peter Jones, businessman and *Dragon's Den* stalwart

Jonathan is one of those rare individuals who has great business acumen as well as entrepreneurial insight. His passion to succeed is infectious.
Mike Clare, founder of Dream Beds plc

Jon is quite simply the most motivated, single-minded and self-believing entrepreneur I have ever met. He will never accept that his goal is unreachable.
Greg Smallwood, investor

ACKNOWLEDGEMENTS

This book is dedicated to my unfaltering wife Lisa and our three special boys: Harry, Fred and Patrick. When your family believe in you, nothing seems impossible.

Thank you also to my dad for your commitment and support, not only during the start-up of the business but for driving me to rugby, helping me with homework and being a great role model throughout my life. I am sure it wasn't always easy. You are doing a great job.

The most valuable piece of advice that I turn to in times of trouble is *"Keep on going"*. Thank you John Handley for your unwavering support. I still remember the first meeting we had in your conservatory that day.

Thank you to all who have helped me in my various endeavours. It would have been impossible without you.

Thank you to all the entrepreneurs, idea generators, risk takers and start-ups. You make the world an amazing place to live and play.

Jonathan Yates, 2009